D1604285

Hereafter

Alan Felsenthal

2024 ✗
8|2

The Song Cave

The Song Cave
www.the-song-cave.com
© 2024, Alan Felsenthal
Cover image: Historic American Buildings Survey, De Peyster, J. W. (1933)
Rose Hill, Woods Road, Tivoli, Dutchess County, NY. Documentation compiled
after 1933. Photograph retrieved from the Library of Congress.

Design and layout by Janet Evans-Scanlon

ISBN: 979-8-9878288-5-4
Library of Congress Control Number: 2024935251

FIRST PRINTING

For sweet William

In memory of
Bob Dellacona
(1945-2021)

I met a magnificent man—
a great spirit who said everything.
Then I wrote these poems.

Contents

III.

Sea, and hill, and wood,
With all the numberless goings-on of life,
Inaudible as dreams!

SAMUEL TAYLOR COLERIDGE,
"FROST AT MIDNIGHT"

I.

ELEGY

Electrolytes are hard to see
though they're everywhere.
Recover quickly
commands the blue bottle.
When will I be able to leave
this planet, you asked. Months
for some, hours for others, I read
in the hospice brochure. The Earth
alights on the edge of the ether. Calcium
in the crust, in the air, in water.
White lines along your shirt
trace where salt left.
The friction we feel between us
and light is darkness, the pain
unable to be untied or loosened.
Minerals obey their crystalline structures.
The soul seeks remission
and requires more.

Untrained augur, the sky is omenless
but it's your duty to look at it.

Under the sun is nothing
at night, the humming-
bird in deep torpor
preserving itself with the stiffness
of a coma. Stationary
or in motion, the force
bonding the universe:
friendship.

In the clearing
a few weeping
trees among the shaded beds
we can see from yours.
Each flicker, cricket, snore
of the pickerel frog, howling
dog you smiled at. A beaver who
kept rebuilding the dam you dismantled
dozes in a hollow warm tonight. Light excels,
splits into a spectrum I see you
through, the saddest optical path.
Other dimensions follow nature
where you will sleep. God
is light you can see
without being consumed.

If you cannot see me, adjust
the lampshade. I may be lost
to blinking electric headlights
bypassing your home.
I recently learned the heart
can beat outside a chest with help
from a machine. The machine
works no harder than it needs to
and I acknowledge its restraint.
Care exhausts me until
I acknowledge everything.

I'm here to make the kettle whistle.
I thought I'd come and give you a look.
The look reserved for visiting hours.
I know clocks die
without help, I'm no longer
afraid of fugitive germs.
Yesterday we learned that suffering
is not only not noble, some people
don't experience it
and what's worse, unless a doctor
tells them, they never know,
and the suffering you're feeling
as I write this won't turn you into
a better person since the bargain
involved with suffering assumes
we all do. We don't.
The unsympathetic winter
gusting through the oldest
white oaks near the Hudson
continues
and so do you
knowing you're cold
while others are less cold
or not cold at all.

You have done your work.
There is no wisdom
where you're headed
—no vexation either.
The bird carries its matter
in its voice. I speak
into a far-off sound.
The loneliest phones don't ring.
Are you at the gate?
Does this key get you out
or keep you in? I say
they should let you leave.
Your host who shows up once
a week left a "comfort
kit" in the fridge
that I called a "clemency box"—
haloperidol, lorazepam,
promethazine, morphine liquid, etc.
The precious ointment is cold.
Who lifts the lid? Let him
now appear.

Windows dim
when you attempt to look through,
doors latch themselves,
the sound sunken
or quiet
except for the owl.
An almond tree we cannot see
with white or pink flowers
grows beyond the window.
There is a shaded street
where a broken wheel
rolls back its way home.
To whom will you return
your spirit? You have proven
the way toward death
is worse than death.
Through the shadow of the Earth
the soul wafts.
I will pay the debts.
Is there anything else?

BEFORE LIGHTHOUSES, GOD WRECKED SHIPS

the passengers turned derelict
soon there was light
you saw this country from the beam
your ship sailed justified by its departure
the captain steered with forehandedness
bore the sea-born breezes
did not fail to sound the signal of fog
the anchor lowered
other anchors would be turned away
when you touched the dock you cried
hid your prayers
later your sons found theirs
the sun abided the days
a cloud of smog lingered
there was no there to return to
there you were
the future was memory
and that was enough for God

IN SILHOUETTE

The ghosts of two workmen who lost their lives to birth the lighthouse roam its hexagonal tomb. Sometimes they ascend the tower to watch for hours as children run and gather sea glass on the shoreline, more than half a mile away. The ghosts cannot clasp hands but look out side by side, their crowns affixed to the arches of the top tier windows, preferring them to rectangular ones below. The children do not overlook the blinking lighthouse; easily seen shooting out mid-sea, it summons them with hints of night. Its melancholy foghorn is said to sound like a juvenile egret drowning with his foot caught in a clam. At sundown clouds shadow the wakes. Through fog the ebb tide carries prayers to the lighthouse, the flood tide trips and burbles in response. Those who don't trust in ghosts claim a "dead man's device" automates the revolving beacon. They're not wrong. Contours of light are solemn, too dignified for living men to bear.

THE BUFFER OF HEDGES

I'm allergic to life in a nutshell

Doctor says

Dreams are antihistamines

When I sneeze

My life is semi-decipherable

Pathways of chamomile

Grow in my thoughts

Though I'm barred from the language

Of fragrance found in gardens

In books I pick up husbandry

From the window I wave

To the next generation of nurserymen

I love the homeliest one

He cannot see me

He hears my cough

Echo through the blinds

COVER LETTER

just say my subject is grief

it comes as a strike
leaves stricken
like an aircraft

afflicted
as Jupiter is
in opposition to Mars

these examples may lead to landing

on the floor
a puddle I try to reconstruct
from willed emotions

don't bother says speech

it's only worry the thing is done
I get along without
the provision of what is unnecessary

prayer all along
hoisting bodies to sky
as they were inhumed

I can keep this up

as long
as death
a book

unreadable from this distance

go try anyway
the rain heaves
something is not shut

the library downstairs only goes to S

DREAMSHIP HELMSMAN

Maria lulls me to slumberland, where I am

charged with sailing a ship with seventeen

thousand children aboard. My first job

after getting a captain's license. I declined

to tell my employer about my narcolepsy.

Instead I decorate the helm's spokes

with bells, so I rouse upon hearing

their rings and arrive in time for the wedding.

OF CLIMBING HEAVEN
AND GAZING ON THE EARTH

Across the waning crescent

as silver pennies drop,

a poppy speaks

to me. What does it say?

What those close to you cannot.

By being pruned one grows

and knows new bulbs: by being

seen one sheds more light

though sometimes disappears.

The moon obscured

like dry sea glass, frosted

by abrasive waves.

A few things stay untouched

by humans after breaking.

Which bottle do you belong to?

I busted mine with the hands

of unexamined life. This phase

makes my dreams lost

to love's treasury. I sleep

under sheets of aluminum,

talking to lunar plants,

having forgotten myself,

unable to speak as I

once did, pallid in the face,

washed-out when blood

moved on. Wearied

by lunar tides, the sea

heaves. I writhe

through memory

like a jerk. It's understandable

why people retire from

the world, reside on the moon,

I just don't know why some

bring the world with them.

II.

GULL ISLAND

In summer the diurnal
laughing gull seeks palms
with crumbs along the beach
his black-hooded head
punctuated by a sharp red beak

that picked shells from the nest
after an egg hatched
in case a shard of shell
settled upon another
prevents hatching of the next

since even a sliver the size
of your thumbnail untrimmed
its weight less than a penny
is too heavy for the pipping
of a chick's egg tooth

under the egg's roof
The parent beak plucks
extracts a foreign grief
so chicks can roughly lift
enough to live

STAY DRY

It's better to want nothing

more than a voice
to say what is sweet
what is sacred

but not what you can't say.

The sky & earth sundered
diamond dust froze
for a child to speak at home.

Say what you must to the house

where your parents live/d
even if it's not the same
door you remember.

The former house hears you

the land remembers all
buildings, homes, temples
and never forgets a foot

that traipsed over its face.

I've forgotten what I said
I wanted to tell you
but no matter

the wind says it for me

the wind says it for you
to know a secret
weather holds.

It's raining again and on

your birthday
droplets are heavy.
Your lover has left you

an umbrella.

IT IS POSSIBLE

they who are
not in love
love none-

theless if
heart-
ache says

and by saying
makes love con-
sequent

on condition
of living
beside an-

other
life
with you

SELF-PORTRAIT

In the ailanthus tree I saw myself

wafting between branches and their

unfallen flowers. I balanced

in the air, perfecting a kind of nonchalance

nobody needs anymore. I lacked the

analogy for what I hadn't felt yet. I tried

to make myself predictable, banal, and

for years was my own analyst. In front

of where I waited I could hear rumbling

like water rushing through a canal. The surge

appeared, I looked into its eye, an exterior

analog of my inner world. Then I knew

my true name was Avalanche.

MEMORY OF THE DEEPS

The moon, never new, is seen

smiling, unlike the deep sea

and its indefinite laugh.

Until we can see the deeps

species exist in dark scenes

smelling bloody water

suctioning each other's heads

spinning slowly through ink

until they bump into what they long for.

The pressure is too high for me

to get there with technology.

The sea doesn't care about my degree.

Nor do creatures for whom I'm food.

Layers below the layers I know

      reveal unimaginable sorrow

if I look at them enough

      to remember stuff I tried to forget.

When I slid down countless fathoms

      my brown eyes exploded

and in my darkened brain

      I was a child again

in the rain looking for facts

      that could bind me to Earth.

I see the moon and the moon sees me,

      God bless the moon and God bless me.

Tides: the moon's dialect

      their rhythm the atlas of time.

Moon appears bounded by the sky

as I am belted with my body

and its desire for water.

Plans to send trash to space

are "nearing attainment."

Soon the moon'll look like Earth.

But not the deep sea so dark

I forget lightness

where dead whales fall

hacksawed

by revolving sleeper sharks.

After my eye explosion

a slight calm subsumed me

so numb I couldn't move.

And before I was eaten

before they could rive flesh from my bones

I considered my first home

    and final bed

my last abyssal zone

    the depressed sea floor

where Hades poses over

    plunging trenches of sediment.

If I can figure out how to live

    with no oxygen present

I might have a chance down here

    where the tallest mountain

stays a mile below the wave's crest.

BOWING TO A CLOUD

mirror-gazing
in low illumination
my friend appeared
apparitions
strange when unexpected
know before you
that you seek them
not as in life
what follows
light
only slight light
softens the world
through vapor
my friend suspended
or diffused by
reality's heat
an evening shadow
trembles
my vision does
when I cut the snuff
from the wick
the sigh of life
separates us

MY ATMOSPHERE

From the green axil of the velvetleaf
angled to the sun and its splintered light
a yellow flower that dulls the green
with its stigma centered in a pistil
opens to acknowledge a social bee.
The cosmopolitan beetle below
senses leaf-mining flies inside the stem.
Born into disturbed soil, this tall weed breathes
by heart-shaped leaves, a stout stalk of soft hairs,
its five petals that converge each summer.
Clouds rend the air, beams extend the sky's dome
and converge in a far vanishing point,
bluish shafts telling us it is twilight,
our gloom. I'd show my son if I had one.

HAPPENING UPON A SCAVENGER HUNT AT THE MUSEUM,

I watched children look at the photographs,
none of them were mine, I did as they did and
spied the shoreline, bright coves, a woodland
or was it a grassland, an oyster pond with nets
resembling lane lines, cormorants perched
by swimming eider ducks, a laughing gull,
silent laugh, the swan carrying her cygnet on
her back, swarms of baby jellyfish at swim,
a lily pad upon which one young painted turtle
delays, a spotted sandpiper standing on a dock
piling that houses periwinkles near dead wakes,
and through the air the imperial moth flies
under the crowned slug, above the diamonds
patterned on the back of a terrapin, the grounded
world written over with the belly of an eastern
ribbon, mounted shadow of a marbled orb weaver's
funnel web, North Star's reflection on the marsh,
a dog's tail splashing in play, a wetland, an osprey,
the ruddy turnstone overturning pebbles, barred
owls, beavers in the seagrass, wild dogs who
paddle through the Sound to snap a nesting swan,
and one kid tee-heed at the mention of a coyote
devouring a watermelon, while a girl wondered
aloud why ospreys clash for shelter with so
many empty houses around.

                                   Any moment
peregrination from home enlarges, as I join
the parade of little strangers, following through
unlocked doors, all safety protocols posted,
my mind a vernal pool for newness to steward.

A MAN AT SEA ON EARTH UNDONE
BY DISTURBANCE WHEN HE APPEARS
MOST ANCHORED

Facts float on
the world we wander
close-winded

Goodness in my worst times
ceases being factual

Good to be good if good is
what you think it means

if you believe you sail
easily old in the soul

But my thoughts heed
images I keep from
friends I've known for ages

Recognition that being unknown
has been my own doing

The ship was mine to drive
signals taken or ignored

Ignoring is not enormity

but wakes a sentence

Say my mind
where stowaways sleep
repeatedly without permission

is the captain's cabin
The hull is built by the patterned ways

I am trying to spy from the starboard
side of my brain by leaving the port

DAYS FLEE FROM GOOD

boundaries of the sea bend
who were people to believe in
oceanfront property
the earth's real message
      it's not about you
benefiting from spring
the beneficiary believes in
earned reality
if you're unhappy
      what have you done
I walk across the mead
the measure of my steps
human chords
when I'm not there
      the field strums its own music
and I'm still mortal
birds eat me before worms
my purpose
      to feed the trees with blood
I watch a single-footed pigeon
mesmerized by a hedgerow
his brother drinks mud
what is it like
      to not believe
world symbols
speak to me

it's never too late for poetry
        until it is
my pastoral doesn't pause
permafrost thaw
        I'm bent on stopping time
mid-infinity
where I am there is
a duration to being
only beings feel
        stones can be hollow
I don't intend to prevent rest
but to lull us
toward a sleep so deep
no alarm ends it
        in which we get to know
wherever dreams lead
where dream is the uniform
we wear to approach
a jury of mirrors
        a storm is on its way
to ask where we went
when the shore met the sea
standing on the sandbank
        blind to the incoming tide

WE LIVE LIKE BOYS WHO DIED

to the pond we go to get frogs
we thought it was a park
at night the gates latch
stones wince at us
we ask each other
if this means we're dead
we lie on graves
eyes shut mouths up
an inch of wind draws dust
on the skin of my palm
how can you know
if breath is real
when it's not cold
helps with a friend
but we both may be dead
and each think we're not
we walk a path we walked
the form of shame is a loop
at dusk we hear a screech
from a beech too far to see
can the dead hear the owl
if we are dead then the dead
hear all we say
but not our thoughts
up high the moon
hard to tell if it has graves too

tough to live on earth
when you think you are dead
dark hours greet dawn
birds prate to the gods
sun breaks the sky
a hole that lets light
dress our mouths our eyes
the dead have no eyes
and we see the sun
we must not be dead
the thought of my pulse
tempts me to leave
to trill or wheeze
my way back to life
life in the air is more
than we can know
so is life in dirt
where worms work a maze
one end is shame
one is grace
too much to think of
our heads have no job
here in this no place
where we came to find frogs
in me a voice pleas
make your heart soft
a place for friends to rest
in books I bond with mates
but you are here with me
a pipe that looks like a bone

frees smoke from the mouth
of an old man on a bench
who feeds young birds with crumbs
he brought from home
like a rite we once did
when we threw bread
from the pier
he may be dead too
the end not far from the start
it is spring
full sun
grass in bloom
blue jays in the shade of a pin oak
fish twist through the pond
our steps on the ground
greet the dead like friends

IMPASSE AT SUNSET

A wish stillness shares,
its matter due with life.
A look betrays light
in a dance. The valley
you roved tracked
by dusk-filled steps.
Trap of nearness,
the knock.
The door, with its clinched
doornail, parts
from the threshold.
The toll awaits.
Step forward, open
the door to lips.
They don't speak.
They kiss.

POEM OF THE POND

Moonless light, the sorrow of listening
to calls of olive frogs, soft, uniform,
their skin damp from hunting speechless snails, slugs,
small lives of the leaf litter. Poets draw

clouds, dirt, mud, night, streams, dawn to tell us how
a goodly, heavy rain washes away,
for a short time, mosquitoes ascending
toward the heavens, their bodies of blood.

They scribble one gesture for the young fox,
impelled to haunt, her soft gray paws stepping
over a thumb-sized hole where white mice hide,
to show us life, alert and destructive.

This old natural lair, this fount of spawn,
an altar upon which relentless gifts
of existence resurge, lift, raise, appear.

But pastoral elegies of this world,
any appetites available here,
can't bring back to us one dear friend now gone.

ORDERING A CASKET
FROM AMAZON PRIME

Avoid cramps by keeping your grip parallel to the hip. 20 gauge steel, but surprisingly light. It's called the *Atlas XL*. You may hear *Atlas* and conjure a collection of maps and charts with his picture as the frontispiece. He is the sea. He is a mountain whose cave shelters the Witch. He fathers nymphs and protects trees. He carries celestial cities on the nape of his neck. Think of the casket as his open palm, cradling your loved one like a precious metal. Consider the sacrifice he makes by using his palm this way. The golden apples are gone; his shoulders heavy; the heavens unheld drop.

THE BORDERLAND OF VISION

A seven-headed serpent
sent to swallow the world
slinks below an angel
to witness the ascent
of an earthy bug
who owned nothing
but a small hard shell
so light it could fit
into your hand as a pick
that strums to the song
the angelic choir sings

SHROUDS WITHOUT POCKETS

Sing psalms to the dolphin
        as he swims north
through ribbons of new blues.

Climb onto his back
        his side fins will act
as stirrups for your feet—

but do not prod him. Let him
        take you from the shore by wind
and misty weather to Neptune

where calm scares the shipwrecked
        and comforts you. Your humble
sea-donkey as he cuts across the invisible

doorframe that smells of white flowers
        where there are none
through disguises of the living world

to the crossroads
        where you'll be held
up again in dreams.

WHAT'S THE PAST LIKE?

Fragments of a water jar restored
with library paste, like cracks

filled and painted over to conceal
a disassembled vessel.

I said I couldn't remember myself,
long ago, fastened long ago,

as a sensitive boy imagining life. But
now I recall the sound a gray bird

made to wake me from a crazed dream.
Like a scratch awl with its fluted wooden

handle chipping bark off an oak tree.
I wrote my name so passersby know

I existed, not who I am. I am a man
now, whatever. I go to town

alone. Time arrested me differently,
its strange sound took custody

of my desire to know myself. It sprained
my ligaments, swelled my back,

and still I ran through the sand dunes
like a wild mare, round-bellied,

and munched on the American beach
grass of forgetfulness. It's hard

to remember that all horses were
once wild. I don't do those things

that I did then. Secrets waver there like
a tail I cannot see. I grew up in a desert

until I was expelled to snowdrifts.
My lexicon, my only friend, was

words the dunes knew, but didn't
say. Memories, primed by westerly

wind, are cold and strong. The wind
shapes the trees, its velocity greets

obliterated landscapes, dead reckoning.
The music of this loamy soil undulates,

a murmur snowballing, and if you can
balance as it trembles, you'll remember

that first sip of gin, of cream, life
when it was dessert. Not an ice floe

begging you to collect its water
and convincing you of its warmth.

IF YOU WANT TO LIVE ALONE
IN A BEE-LOUD GLADE

leave the grass
uncut
grown to meadow
or cut fewer times
each year
the wild bees
increase
and not far off
a bobolink
where one never was
reposes on an
unmarked
headstone
breeze enlivens
the field
a slight summer
cooling
I sit on steps of
a family
mausoleum
whose history
I don't know
the past seated
with me
unacknowledged

not that it needs to be

bees vibrate across
the meadow
bats sleep
in a tree's cradle
at night
the unseen speaks
a tawny owl
hidden from vision
I am night-blind
I don't know
history
what I know
doesn't decrease
the bereaved
the world
subleased
the bees
are squatters
who pay
honey
without meaning to
people buried here
bought their plots

beyond
the brownstone gates
the west is
behind us

green monk
parakeets above
mimic
speech
no one owns
what comes after
the meadow groans
weeping
beech trees
the rain roughens
white marble
carved to resemble
kneeling angels
their sugaring skins
dissolving
small crystals

a new sound
the bees emit
pollinating
or caught in
a spider's web
pitches shift
limbed-up
maples
line the roadway
to the crematorium
ash lands
on a banker's tongue
who doesn't notice

its passing
few
versions of life are
achievable
taller grasses
bear fruit
proceed close
by them
to us
they don't belong

EARTHWARD

Mourners in sunken light
of the cypress magnified
the sensitivity of dew

Moths withdrew from the olive tree
into ashy distances

The mourners ambled
until nothing threatening
tended to them

They wore the aura of dole
only animals sense

Coursing low a rare vagrant
splintered the mouse skull
with a hooked bill

The authors of destruction
esteem its skeletal forms

I can be honest in my dreams
but I know almost nothing
of deep sleep

THE HAWK AT
WASHINGTON SQUARE PARK

Set on a wire, on a breezeless
day, his frame was
a figurine that stared at us.
People, eyes on each other, pass.
The majestic sentinel sits
slightly above our bitterness,
his body its own crutch. He is
proving the true nature of his
greatness by being ignored. As
if saying, impassively, be noiseless,
unseen, not behind or under us—
you belong to your times—
but above, commit to spirit, yours.
And then a gentle wind comes.

III.

IS MY HIGHER SOUL SPEAKING?

The spellbinder
childhood mind was
when we
whispered behind paper masks
when we
faced east without knowing
Could be the invisible forest
       surrounded our family tree
Could be
what we
longed for
our neighbors had
            respondence
The contrivance of warning
invented my need to
design facts
a mind of knowledge indestructible
to father the central fire
to discharge
luminously
thought as a weapon

At school drills reinvented fire
I wired shells to a tray
not stamps
flowers too fragrant
stones reminded me of loneliness
Hold this poem to a comb
hum it into a kazoo
Thrushes sing
mallards swim
crows caw overhead
the catbird mews
Do I know three bird songs
            Do I know one
Paper and string marry into
a fork-tailed kite
I might've flown in
the screeching wind
A spruce is a pine of paper

I looped two
ropes to paint cans
walked over puddles
          trails
translated by angered parents
A simple voltaic cell
our doorbell rings
answer with your world badge
under your left pocket
My heart
an attic full of loose papers
the old frayed
wire from a den lamp
oily rags
know your exit
Dead branches as faulty truss bridges
Trees sigh as I do
Youth
a sideshow ended
Adulthood
the study of rhythmics

What is the death knell sound
The swans without words
sky tightens its belt
Now is for a bird I haven't met
        ungoogleable
Invent his chirp
If I cannot find the knowledge
the house burns down the school
burns all the books burn
Which is the knowledge angel
How to treat heart wounds
with a window plant
It was hard to learn
the word *copse*
        after *corpse*

Bury me with my books
collected on my tomb's behalf
so many I'm unsure
              where the body goes
I want all the knowledge but am
unhappy the more I receive
Is it better to be a rich man's
son or a wise man's
I've met men who believe DNA
others who say
angels instruct our fates
The breeze prevails
Bury me somewhere I can stink
without being
ashamed
Do bones rust
              They must
Do they crumble with decay
That too

How do you do
        what you need to
with what you've done
I went to the Salton Sea I was young
with a boy of twenty
years ago
My footsteps crackled
I said to the boy
        This is the loudest sand
He was already a man
I thought of as a boy
though he was 6 feet tall
That's not sand it's fish
        bones
He told me
the history of the Salton Sea
dream of a desert resort
the eye of Heaven didn't share
Don't look it up
I'll tell you someday when we're
not already sad

We hiked Joshua Tree and he
gathered sage to sell
at a tea garden on Melrose
We slept in the same tent
I was asleep when I touched him
he said the next morning
Across from the garden was
a bookstore named after a tree
with an annex of used books
I hoarded its knowledge
doubling volumes on the Billy
bookshelves in my apartment
Reading I'd soon forget
not enough to admit stupidity
calling it "processing" "working
          thru it"
Fine wires
It's the knowledge
I'm more lightweight than I meant to be
          that sits on my head like hair
Felt like experience
was the inedible core
some fruit greeted us with
If we think man a batch of matter
we grew up to be computers
Now you know how
my memory stores

The mind's the soul's landlord
No wonder the soul moves on
Its quest to live a poem
Angels belong to Rilke
Satan Milton
what's left for you in the 2020s
Leaves speak
Trees write their most
potent verse
underground
their lines communicate water
Grafting goes with
          love
I was weaned on poetry
that pissed on the grave of language
          But no plot exists
for what can't be said
Yearning to transmute feeling
can fail meaningfully
How to avoid being
Rilke's echo
Mechanically
to repeat without mind
particleboard

Mind flogs the heart
How can the heart tend
a garden in our time
The green thumb in a
thumbscrew as the earth melts
Climate waterboarded the world
          and we're Climate
To no longer use "interrogate"
in artist statements
To no longer use "waterboard"
          as metaphor
Does God plead the case
without arriving
The mosquito buzz above my bed
indistinguishable from breath
Nowhere
under a sheet to hide
Into what I try to obscure
a beak
peaks in
The higher I ascend fewer
molecules to breathe
An angel is made of pressurized
air for flight
How
can I see your heart
I can't even see gravity

Here's a fact
George de Mestral invented Velcro
out of cockleburs
Some seeds sow themselves
The trick of the tree was poison
          they told us
Sinking deeper into life
bodies turn earth like oat drills
Try it without facts
Whisper when leafless
Brew remedy for the Salton Sea
Turn whichever way isn't asked for
          Forgive yourself
in the basement looking down
wondering if the center exists
The world lives
Plato
said so
the stars and Saturn
but that was when we
only had five planets
As a boy I visited the stars' zoo
Countless eyes gazed back
without judgment
Seen is different than visible
          No demon told me this
the angels already knew
The eyelid of paradise opens

I go into
vision where
I could stay if I didn't
believe in dreams

The epicenter of pain
        moves
through continents years
disappears the center of
the world equidistant to
wherever you're standing
while considering ancestors
Did they think of this poem for you
on the ship from Hell
And what did they glean
in the New World
Not the knotted money tree
I was lucky to find my willow
The winters dormant
        but my toes grew

The mind's archive
            run by interns
So many gaps in what I need
to know to know how
to say what
I want
There is birdsong only
birds can hear
            filled with answers
I may need
What is the opposite of breathe
Open the windows
to make
your house a chime
wind plays

The air dressed up in prayer
has no age
carries bliss
and in the same
gust sadness
I may stay a child even
after pilgrimage
after
ancestry
lessons in the years
the herbs burnt
How am I living
what have I earned

Notes

1. The title "OF CLIMBING HEAVEN AND GAZING ON THE EARTH" is from Percy Bysshe Shelley's "To the Moon":

Art thou pale for weariness
Of climbing Heaven, and gazing on the earth,
Wandering companionless
Among the stars that have a different birth,—
And ever changing, like a joyless eye
That finds no object worth its constancy?

2. "GULL ISLAND" is for Betty Chen.

3. The title "IF YOU WANT TO LIVE ALONE IN A BEE-LOUD GLADE" borrows from the first stanza of William Butler Yeats's "The Lake Isle of Innisfree":

I will arise and go now, and go to Innisfree,
And a small cabin build there, of clay and wattles made;
Nine bean-rows will I have there, a hive for the honey-bee,
And live alone in the bee-loud glade.

Acknowledgments

I would like to thank the editors of the following publications, where versions of these poems first appeared: *The Baffler, Critical Quarterly, Fence, Literary Hub, New York Review of Books, On the Seawall, Oversound, Poetry Salzburg Review,* and *Rainbow Agate.*

Some of the poems in this book were written while in residence at Lighthouse Works on Fishers Island, NY. Thank you to the people who made that possible for me: Tryn Collins, Claudia DeSimone, and Nate Malinowski.

Many friends helped bring these poems to life: Ari Banias, Dan Beachy-Quick, Mermer Blakeslee, Hannah Brooks-Motl, Farnoosh Fathi, Mary Gossy, Sam Grossman, Patricia Spears Jones, Ben Lerner, Emily Sieu Liebowitz, Amanda Nadelberg, Sara Nicholson, Alice Notley, Geoffrey G. O'Brien, Ariana Reines, and Chase Twichell.

Many thanks to Michael Silverblatt for decades of conversation, encouragement, and friendship.

Special thanks to my dear friend and longtime co-editor, Ben Estes, without whom The Song Cave would not exist.

This book is dedicated to my beloved—William Penrose—in memory of Bob Dellacona, both of whom I needed in order to write these poems.

Thank you to my family, especially my parents, for their support.

And thank you, dear reader, for making it here.

OTHER TITLES FROM THE SONG CAVE: